Instant Testing with CasperJS

Create advanced and efficient CasperJS tests for your web development projects

Éric Bréhault

BIRMINGHAM - MUMBAI

Instant Testing with CasperJS

First published: January 2014

Production Reference: 1230114

Published by Packt Publishing Ltd.
Livery Place
35 Livery Street
Birmingham B3 2PB, UK.

ISBN 978-1-78328-943-1

www.packtpub.com

Credits

Author
Éric Bréhault

Reviewer
Sven Anders Robbestad

Acquisition Editors
Pramila Balan
Harsha Bharwani

Commissioning Editor
Govindan K

Technical Editors
Veena Pagare
Manal Pednekar

Copy Editors
Insiya Morbiwala
Stuti Srivastava

Project Coordinators
Sherin Padayatty
Sageer Parkar

Proofreaders
Simran Bhogal
Paul Hindle

Production Coordinator
Nilesh Bambardekar

Cover Work
Valentina D'silva

About the Author

Éric Bréhault wrote his very first web pages in 1993, started JavaScript application development in 1998, and is still enjoying it.

As an IT engineer, he has used a lot of different server-side technologies, but since 2006, he has been focusing on Plone—a Python open source CMS—and been an active participant of its community. His main contribution has probably been Plomino, a Plone-based application builder. He has also worked on different, modern web mapping solutions such as Leaflet.

JavaScript has always been an important part of his work, and he started using CasperJS in 2012 as his favorite testing utility. He developed Resurrectio, a CasperJS test recorder Chrome extension.

He works as a technical manager at Makina Corpus—a French open source consulting and development company providing services for web and mobile applications—specifically on environmental issues and in the fields of spatial analysis and data visualization.

I would like to thank all my teachers.

About the Reviewer

Sven Anders Robbestad is a software developer with extensive experience in web technologies. He is also an experienced developer of mobile apps for phones and tablets. Primarily experienced in the field of machine learning and web intelligence, he currently resides in Norway where he works at a senior level at SOL.no.

www.PacktPub.com

Support files, eBooks, discount offers and more

You might want to visit www.PacktPub.com for support files and downloads related to your book.

Did you know that Packt offers eBook versions of every book published, with PDF and ePub files available? You can upgrade to the eBook version at www.PacktPub.com and as a print book customer, you are entitled to a discount on the eBook copy. Get in touch with us at service@packtpub.com for more details.

At www.PacktPub.com, you can also read a collection of free technical articles, sign up for a range of free newsletters and receive exclusive discounts and offers on Packt books and eBooks.

http://PacktLib.PacktPub.com

Do you need instant solutions to your IT questions? PacktLib is Packt's online digital book library. Here, you can access, read and search across Packt's entire library of books.

Why Subscribe?

- ▸ Fully searchable across every book published by Packt
- ▸ Copy and paste, print and bookmark content
- ▸ On demand and accessible via web browser

Free Access for Packt account holders

If you have an account with Packt at www.PacktPub.com, you can use this to access PacktLib today and view nine entirely free books. Simply use your login credentials for immediate access.

Table of Contents

Preface

CasperJS is a fantastic command-line utility offering a wide JavaScript API to script and test any web page. Unlike Selenium, CasperJS does not automate a locally installed web browser; it behaves as an actual independent web browser.

To automate a locally installed web browser, CasperJS uses PhantomJS, which is a headless WebKit engine. Well, "headless WebKit engine" might sound like quite a barbaric term, but just imagine this as a WebKit engine (the famous web engine of Chrome and Safari) without a graphical user interface.

So it is basically a web browser. It can load web pages, apply their CSS, run their JavaScript, interact with their content, and so on; but when we launch it from a command line, we do not see anything on the screen.

Instead of a standard graphical user interface, PhantomJS offers a JavaScript API so we can control what the browser is doing. By running its own web engine instead of automating an external web browser, PhantomJS is much faster and lighter than Selenium.

Unfortunately, the PhantomJS JavaScript API is very low level. So by writing a simple interaction scenario rapidly, you could end up with quite a heavy and long script code.

This is precisely where CasperJS makes its entrance. It comes with two precious assets. Firstly, with a large, high-level API to perform actions such as clicking links, filling forms, and finding elements; and secondly, with the ability to execute those actions sequentially without requiring an endless cascade of JavaScript callbacks.

Thanks to this, our CasperJS scripts will be just as concise and readable as we wish, which is priceless when dealing with testing.

CasperJS was created by Nicolas Perriault in 2011, and he is still actively maintaining it. All the CasperJS users are very grateful for it. Thank you Nicolas!

What this book covers

Installing CasperJS (Simple) explains how to properly install PhantomJS and CasperJS plus their system dependencies needed on our machine, step by step.

Getting started with CasperJS (Simple) covers how to write basic CasperJS tests. Starting with simple scripts, we will progressively get familiar with the CasperJS approach, discover what kind of assertions can be performed with CasperJS, learn how to establish the proper timing to get an accurate test, and how to record a web session as a CasperJS script.

Writing advanced tests (Intermediate) details how to simulate rich web interactions using CasperJS in order to achieve more complex testing, such as handling files, managing authentication, or simulating keyboard and mouse events efficiently.

Best practices (Intermediate) focuses on making our tests more accurate and robust and explains how to run them using continuous integration (CI) tools, such as Jenkins or Travis CI.

Beyond testing (Advanced) discusses other interesting CasperJS usages such as web scripting and automated screenshot or server-side printing.

What you need for this book

To execute the examples contained in this book, you will need a computer compatible with Windows, Mac OS X, or Linux, with sufficient rights to be able to install new software.

Who this book is for

This book assumes that you are familiar with web development and have a good knowledge of JavaScript.

Conventions

In this book, you will find a number of styles of text that distinguish between different kinds of information. Here are some examples of these styles, and an explanation of their meaning.

Code words in text are shown as follows: "We can print log messages using the `log` method."

A block of code is set as follows:

```
casper.start('http://en.wikipedia.org/', function() {
    this.echo(this.getCurrentUrl());
});
```

When we wish to draw your attention to a particular part of a code block, the relevant lines or items are set in bold:

```
casper.start('http://en.wikipedia.org/', function() {
    this.echo(this.getCurrentUrl());
});
```

Any command-line input or output is written as follows:

```
~ casperjs test.js
```

New terms and **important words** are shown in bold. Words that you see on the screen, in menus or dialog boxes for example, appear in the text like this: "It shows a **Click me** button, and if we click on it, its label is changed to **Done**."

Warnings or important notes appear in a box like this.

Tips and tricks appear like this.

Reader feedback

Feedback from our readers is always welcome. Let us know what you think about this book—what you liked or may have disliked. Reader feedback is important for us to develop titles that you really get the most out of.

To send us general feedback, simply send an e-mail to `feedback@packtpub.com`, and mention the book title via the subject of your message.

If there is a topic that you have expertise in and you are interested in either writing or contributing to a book, see our author guide on `www.packtpub.com/authors`.

Customer support

Now that you are the proud owner of a Packt book, we have a number of things to help you to get the most from your purchase.

Downloading the example code

You can download the example code files for all Packt books you have purchased from your account at `http://www.PacktPub.com`. If you purchased this book elsewhere, you can visit `http://www.PacktPub.com/support` and register to have the files e-mailed directly to you.

Errata

Although we have taken every care to ensure the accuracy of our content, mistakes do happen. If you find a mistake in one of our books—maybe a mistake in the text or the code—we would be grateful if you would report this to us. By doing so, you can save other readers from frustration and help us improve subsequent versions of this book. If you find any errata, please report them by visiting `http://www.packtpub.com/support`, selecting your book, clicking on the **errata submission form** link, and entering the details of your errata. Once your errata are verified, your submission will be accepted and the errata will be uploaded on our website, or added to any list of existing errata, under the Errata section of that title. Any existing errata can be viewed by selecting your title from `http://www.packtpub.com/support`.

Piracy

Piracy of copyright material on the Internet is an ongoing problem across all media. At Packt, we take the protection of our copyright and licenses very seriously. If you come across any illegal copies of our works, in any form, on the Internet, please provide us with the location address or website name immediately so that we can pursue a remedy.

Please contact us at `copyright@packtpub.com` with a link to the suspected pirated material.

We appreciate your help in protecting our authors, and our ability to bring you valuable content.

Questions

You can contact us at `questions@packtpub.com` if you are having a problem with any aspect of the book, and we will do our best to address it.

Instant Testing with CasperJS

Welcome to *Instant Testing with CasperJS*. This book will cover how to practice efficient and solid web page testing using CasperJS. CasperJS is a cross-platform, command-line utility that is able to load and script any web page.

Installing CasperJS (Simple)

In this recipe, we will cover the steps to install CasperJS and its dependencies on Windows, Mac OS X, and Linux.

Getting ready

The CasperJS sources are managed on GitHub. So, to get them on our local machine, we need Git.

To install Git on Windows, we can use msysGit to deploy the Git command-line utility plus a graphical interface:

1. Go to `http://msysgit.github.io/`.
2. Go to the **Downloads** page.
3. Download the latest version.
4. Run the installer.

To install Git on Mac, the easiest way is to use Git for OS X graphical interface:

1. Go to `https://code.google.com/p/git-osx-installer/`.
2. Go to the **Downloads** page.
3. Download the latest version.
4. Run the installer.

You can also install Git from the MacPorts:

1. Make sure MacPorts is installed (if not, go to `http://www.macports.org/` and follow the instructions).
2. From a command line, enter the following command:

   ```
   $ sudo port install git-core +svn +doc +bash_completion +gitweb
   ```

To install Git on Linux, use the following commands:

- For Debian/Ubuntu, enter the following command:

  ```
  $ sudo apt-get install git
  ```

- For Fedora, enter the following command:

  ```
  $ yum install git-core
  ```

How to do it...

1. First of all, we need to install PhantomJS.

   Perform the following steps to install PhantomJS on Windows:

   1. Go to `http://phantomjs.org/download.html`.
   2. Download the Windows version.
   3. Extract its content.
   4. Add the `phantomjs.exe` path to the `PATH` environment variable, assuming it is located at `C:\PhantomJS`:

      ```
      ...the existing PATH value...;C:\PhantomJS
      ```

   Perform the following steps to install PhantomJS on Mac and Linux:

   1. Go to `http://phantomjs.org/download.html`.
   2. Download the appropriate version (Mac OS X / Linux 32 bits / Linux 64 bits).
   3. Extract its content.

4. Make `bin/phamtomjs` available in your system path using the following command:

```
~ sudo ln -s <path-to-extracted-folder>/bin/phantomjs /usr/local/bin
```

Now we should be able to run `phantomjs` from a command line:

```
~ phantomjs --version
1.9.0
```

2. Now, we can install CasperJS using Git. We need to locally clone the official CasperJS repository from GitHub.

   This can be achieved using the following command:

```
~ git clone git://github.com/n1k0/casperjs.git
```

   This should produce an output similar to the following command:

```
Cloning into 'casperjs'...
remote: Counting objects: 11156, done.
remote: Compressing objects: 100% (4927/4927), done.
remote: Total 11156 (delta 6580), reused 10692 (delta 6167)
Receiving objects: 100% (11156/11156), 6.85 MiB | 113 KiB/s, done.
Resolving deltas: 100% (6580/6580), done.
```

3. To check out the last stable version, we need to run the following Git command:

```
~ git checkout tags/1.1-beta3
```

   We will get the following message:

```
Note: checking out 'tags/1.1-beta3'.
```

```
..
```

```
HEAD is now at bc0da16... bump 1.1-beta3
```

4. Let's check if CasperJS is properly installed.

   To check if CasperJS is installed properly on Windows, use the following commands:

```
~ cd casperjs
~ bin\batchbin\casperjs.bat --version
```

To check if CasperJS is installed properly on Mac OS X / Linux, use the following commands:

```
~ cd ./casperjs
~ bin/casperjs --version
```

We should obtain the following result:

```
1.1.0-beta3
```

5. To complete the installation, we will now make sure that the `casperjs` executable is available in our system path.

    To complete the installation on Windows add the following path to `casperjs.bat` to the `PATH` environment variable, assuming the repository is located in `C:\casperjs`:

    ```
    ...the existing PATH value...;C:\casperjs\batchbin
    ```

    To complete the installation on Mac and Linux, link `bin/casperjs` in `/usr/local/bin` using the following command:

    ```
    ~ sudo ln -s `pwd`/bin/casperjs /usr/local/bin
    ```

    We can check if `casperjs` is in the system path using the following command:

    ```
    ~ casperjs --version
    1.1.0-beta3
    ```

The setup is now complete.

How it works...

Just after cloning the repository, we launched a Git command to get the Version 1.1 (which was still a beta version at the time we were writing those lines).

If we had not launched the Git command, we would still have had a correct CasperJS setup, but be careful; Git has downloaded all the CasperJS revisions since the very beginning of CasperJS's development till today, and *has automatically checked out the last one*. So, we try using the following command:

```
~ bin/casperjs --version
```

We will obtain something similar to the following result:

```
1.1.0-DEV
```

It means that we are running the current development version and using a development version is probably not what we want as it might be unstable or even broken.

That is why we need to check out the 1.1 tagged revision specifically.

There's more...

Now, let's discuss some installation options.

Installing CasperJS with Homebrew on Mac OS X

Homebrew is a package manager for Mac OS X. It is a very handy way to deploy PhantomJS and CasperJS using the following command:

```
~ brew install casperjs
```

Installing PhantomJS on Ubuntu

Be careful; on Ubuntu, if we install PhantomJS from the distribution packages, we will get an old version (Version 1.4 or 1.6, depending on our Ubuntu version).

But CasperJS needs at least PhantomJS 1.7. So, package installation is not an option.

Using the CasperJS Ruby executable

On Mac OS X and Linux, the default `casperjs` executable is a Python script. Python should be available on our system (unless we use an exotic Linux distribution), so it makes no problem.

Nevertheless, if we prefer to launch CasperJS using a Ruby script, we do have one in `./rubybin`. So, we just need to make it available in our system path this way:

```
~ ln -sf `pwd`/rubybin/casperjs /usr/local/bin/casperjs
```

Getting started with CasperJS (Simple)

This recipe will explain how to write basic CasperJS tests and will help us get familiar with the CasperJS approach.

Getting ready

In this recipe, we will build simple web pages in order to run our CasperJS tests in an appropriate context.

As we need to serve just static content (HTML, CSS, JavaScript), we need a very basic HTTP server and the simplest existing HTTP server is the Python 2 SimpleHTTPServer, as it is part of the standard Python installation (so that no extra deployment is needed), and it does not need any system configuration.

On Mac OS X and Linux, Python 2 is part of the system; we just launch the following command line from the folder containing our web content:

```
~ python -m SimpleHTTPServer
```

The preceding command should return this message:

```
Serving HTTP on 0.0.0.0 port 8000 …
```

The message means that our local web server is running on the `8000` port and we can access it with our web browser using the following URL:

```
http://localhost:8000/
```

On Windows, we can do the very same thing but Python is not installed by default, so we first need to install it this way:

1. Go to `http://www.python.org/getit/`.
2. Download the Python 2.7 Windows installer.
3. Run it.
4. Add Python to our system path:

   ```
   ...the existing PATH value...;C:\Python27\
   ```

How to do it...

We are now ready to write CasperJS tests. For our first test, we will not need our local web server as we will use the Wikipedia website:

1. Let's create the following file and name it `example1.js`:

   ```javascript
   var casper = require('casper').create();

   casper.start('http://en.wikipedia.org/', function() {
       this.echo(this.getTitle());
   });

   casper.run();
   ```

2. When we run our script, we get the following output:

```
~ casperjs example1.js
Wikipedia, the free encyclopedia
~
```

3. Let's see how it works:
   - In the first line, we get a new `'casper'` instance.
   - Then, in the second line, we start this instance and open the Wikipedia page.
   - We give the `start()` method a function that will be executed once the page is loaded. In this function, the context (`this`) is the `casper` instance. Here, we just use the `echo()` method to display the current page title (obtained using `getTitle()`).
   - In the last line, we launch the registered steps.

Now, let's change a little bit of our script in order to perform a search on Wikipedia about `'javascript'`:

```javascript
var casper = require('casper').create();

casper.start('http://en.wikipedia.org/', function() {
    this.echo(this.getTitle());
    this.fill('form#searchform', {
        'search': 'javascript'
    }, true);
});

casper.then(function() {
    this.echo(this.getCurrentUrl());
})

casper.run();
```

4. Let's run it:

```
~ casperjs example1.js
Wikipedia, the free encyclopedia
http://en.wikipedia.org/wiki/Javascript
~
```

We have made two changes:

- ❑ We used the `fill()` method to submit our search keyword to the Wikipedia search form
- ❑ We added a new step in our script using the `then()` method to make sure that we wait for the search result to be returned; we also displayed the current URL

As we can see, it works perfectly as we obtained the URL of the Wikipedia article about JavaScript. Now, let's "assert" the world!

We just wrote a basic CasperJS script, but it is not a very efficient test script as a test script is supposed to check if an expected behavior is properly performed by the web page that we are testing.

To do that, CasperJS provides a tester API, which can be accessed via the `test` property of our CasperJS instance.

5. Let's create the following example page and name it `example2.html`:

```html
<html><body>
    <button id="button1" onclick="this.innerText='Done';">Click
me</button>
</body></html>
```

Now, let's launch our SimpleHTTPServer and see what the page looks like by going to `http://localhost:8000/example2.html`.

It shows a **Click me** button and if we click on it, its label is changed to **Done**.

6. The following is a CasperJS test that could validate this behavior:

```javascript
casper.test.begin('Test my form', 3, function(test) {
    casper.start('http://localhost:8000/example2.html', function()
{
        test.assertVisible("button#button1");
        test.assertSelectorHasText("button#button1", "Click me");
    });

    casper.then(function() {
        this.click("button#button1");
    });

    casper.then(function() {
      test.assertSelectorHasText("button#button1", "Done");
    })

    casper.run(function() {
        test.done();
    });
});
```

7. Let's save this script as `example2.js` and run it using the `casperjs test` command:

```
~ casperjs test example2.js
Test file: example2.js
# Test my form
PASS Selector is visible
PASS Found "Click me" within the selector "button#button1"
PASS Found "Done" within the selector "button#button1"
PASS 3 tests executed in 0.095s, 3 passed, 0 failed, 0 dubious, 0 skipped.
~
```

The `casperjs test` command allows us to use the `casper.test` property, which provides all the testing methods.

When using the `casperjs test` command, we do not need to create the `casper` instance, but we need to call the `begin` method and end the test with the `done` method.

8. First, with `assertVisible`, we make sure that our button is visible. The most common way to designate an element is by providing an accurate CSS selector.

9. Then, we use `assertSelectorHasText` to check the text content of the button before and after clicking on it. We can see that all our tests pass.

The `begin` method takes a description and the number of expected tests (beside the test itself) as parameters. The number of successful and failed tests are displayed in the final line.

10. Now, let's break our tests by changing the second `assertSelectorHasText` tester as shown in the following code:

```
this.test.assertSelectorHasText("button#button1", "You can click
again");
```

Downloading the example code

You can download the example code files for all Packt books you have purchased from your account at `http://www.PacktPub.com`. If you purchased this book elsewhere, you can visit `http://www.PacktPub.com/support` and register to have the files e-mailed directly to you.

11. And the result is as follows:

```
~ casperjs test example2.js
Test file: example2.js
# Test my form
PASS Selector is visible
FAIL Found "You can click again" within the selector "button#button1"
#    type: assertSelectorHasText
#    file: example2.js:4
#    code: test.assertSelectorHasText("button#button1", "You can click again");
#    subject: false
#    selector: "button#button1"
#    text: "You can click again"
#    actualContent: "Click me"
PASS Found "Done" within the selector "button#button1"
FAIL 3 tests executed in 0.12s, 2 passed, 1 failed, 0 dubious, 0 skipped.

Details for the 1 failed test:

In example2.js:4
  Test my form
    assertSelectorHasText: Found "You can click again" within the selector "butto
n#button1"
~
```

We clearly see that our two assertions still pass, but one is now failing.

Timing is everything

When developing with JavaScript, we often need to chain two pieces of code (for instance, first we load some JSON data, then we update the page content using that data). But, each step is generally non-blocking, which means that the rest of the code will continue to execute even if the step is not complete, and there is no way to predict when the first step will be complete.

The most solid and common approach to solve this problem is the *callback* mechanism. We put the second piece of code in a function and pass it as a parameter to the first one, so that it can call that function when it finishes.

As a result, there is no linear and predictably-ordered execution of the code. This makes testing a little bit tricky.

The following is an example (example3.html):

```html
<html>
<head>
    <script type='text/javascript' src='http://code.jquery.com/jquery-
1.9.1.js'></script>
    <style>
    .searching { color: grey;}
    .success { color: green;}
    .noresults {color: red;}
    </style>
```

```html
</head>
<body>
    <script>
    function geonamesSearch() {
        $('#results').html("Searching...");
        $('#results').attr('class', 'searching');
        var url = "http://api.geonames.org/searchJSON";
        var query = $('#searchedlocation').val();
          $.getJSON(url + "?username=demo&q="+ query
          +"&maxRows=25&featureClass=P",null,
              function(data) {
                  var data = data.geonames;
                  var names = [];
                  if(data.length > 0) {
                      $.each(data, function(i, val){
                          names.push(val.name +" ("+val.adminName1+")");
                      });
                      $('#results').html(names.join("<br/>"));
                      $('#results').attr('class', 'success');
                  } else {
                      $('#results').html("No matching place.");
                      $('#results').attr('class', 'noresults');
                  }
              }
          );
    }
    </script>
    <input type="text" id="searchedlocation" />
    <button id="search" onclick="geonamesSearch();">Click me</button>
    <div id="results"></div>
</body>
</html>
```

The demo account we are using here to access the Geonames.org service has a daily limit, if the limit is reached, we can go `http://www.geonames.org/login` and create our own account. The preceding code will create a page that contains a text input field, a button, and an empty div with an ID as `'results'`. When we click on the button, the JavaScript function `geonamesSearch` does the following:

- It puts the `'searching'` class on the `results` div and inserts the **Searching...** mention

- It reads the text input's current value

- It calls the GeoNames JSON web services to get the place names matching the value that you input

- ▶ This JSON call is performed by jQuery and we provide it with a callback function that will be called when the GeoNames web service will respond and read the results

- ▶ If there is no result, it changes the `results` div class to `'noresults'` and its text to **No matching place.**

- ▶ If there are some results, it sets the class to `'success'` and displays the matching place names

We can try it with our web browser and see it work nicely.

Now, let's test this page with the following script (`example3.js`), which enters the value `'barcelona'` and asserts that we do get **Barcelona (Catalonia)** in the results:

```
casper.userAgent('Mozilla/5.0 (Macintosh; Intel Mac OS X)');

casper.test.begin('Search a city by name', 1, function(test) {
    casper.start('http://localhost:8000/example3.html', function() {
        this.sendKeys("input#searchedlocation", "barcelona");
        this.click("button#search");
    });

    casper.then(function() {
        test.assertTextExists('Barcelona (Catalonia)', 'Barcelona
(Catalonia) has been found.');
    })

    casper.run(function() {
        test.done();
    });
});
```

> We need to set up a regular user agent to make sure that `geonames.org` will accept to process our request.

If we run it, we get a failure:

```
~ casperjs test example3.js
Test file: example3.js
# Search a city by name
FAIL Barcelona (Catalonia) has been found.
#    type: assertTextExists
#    file: example3.js:11
#    code: test.assertTextExists('Barcelona (Catalonia)', 'Barcelona (Catalonia)
has been found.');
#    subject: false
#    text: "Barcelona (Catalonia)"
FAIL 1 test executed in 0.992s, 0 passed, 1 failed, 0 dubious, 0 skipped.

Details for the 1 failed test:

In example3.js:11
   Search a city by name
     assertTextExists: Barcelona (Catalonia) has been found.
~
```

Why is that? Because our `this.click()` triggers the `geonamesSearch` function and immediately after that we try to assert the result content. However, as the GeoNames web service did not have enough time to respond, the content is not yet the one expected at the time the assertion is performed.

To manage these kinds of cases, CasperJS offers us the ability to wait before executing the rest of our tests.

The following is a working test script:

```javascript
casper.userAgent('Mozilla/5.0 (Macintosh; Intel Mac OS X)');

casper.test.begin('Search a city by name', 1, function(test) {
    casper.start('http://localhost:8000/example3.html', function() {
        this.sendKeys("input#searchedlocation", "barcelona");
        this.click("button#search");
    });

    casper.waitForSelector('div.success', function() {
        test.assertTextExists('Barcelona (Catalonia)', 'Barcelona
(Catalonia) has been found.');
    })

    casper.run(function() {
        test.done();
    });
});
```

We can see that the tests pass successfully now:

```
~ casperjs test example3.js
Test file: example3.js
# Search a city by name
PASS Barcelona (Catalonia) has been found.
PASS 1 test executed in 1.301s, 1 passed, 0 failed, 0 dubious, 0 skipped.
~
```

With `waitForSelector`, we make sure that the assertion will be performed only when the `results` div will have the `'success'` class, and it will happen only once our JSON loading callback function has been called.

> The `waitForSelector` method will not wait forever; it does have a timeout (with a default value of 5000 milliseconds, which can be changed) and we can provide a second function that will be called if the timeout is reached before the selector is satisfied.

Live recording

Writing tests can take time. A quick and convenient way to produce tests is to record an actual usage sequence directly from our web browser (just like the Firefox Selenium plug-in).

To record web sequences as CasperJS tests, we can use a Chrome extension named **Resurrectio**.

We install it from the Chrome Web Store (go to `https://chrome.google.com/webstore/`, search for `resurrectio`, and then click on the add button), and it just appends a new button next to the URL bar:

1. We click on the **Resurrectio** button to start a recording:

2. We can then navigate or perform any regular action in our window.

3. By right-clicking, we can add some assertions or screenshots:

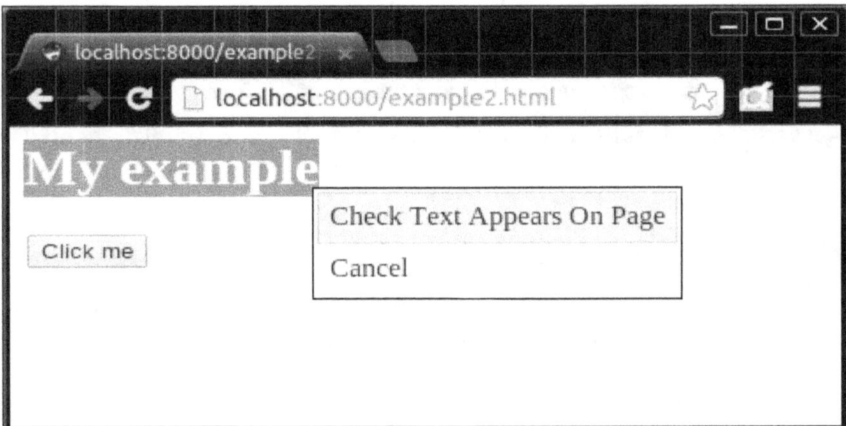

4. By clicking again on the **Resurrectio** button, we can stop the recording and then export the previous sequence as a a CasperJS test:

```javascript
//=============================================================
// Casper generated Tue Jun 11 2013 19:57:56 GMT+0200 (CEST)
//=============================================================

var x = require('casper').selectXPath;
var casper = require('casper').create();
casper.options.viewportSize = {width: 674, height: 431};
casper.start('http://localhost:8000/example2.html');
casper.waitForSelector(x("//*[contains(text(), 'My example')]"),
    function success() {
        this.test.assertExists(x("//*[contains(text(), 'My example')]"));
      },
    function fail() {
        this.test.assertExists(x("//*[contains(text(), 'My example')]"));
});
casper.waitForSelector("form button#button1",
    function success() {
        this.test.assertExists("form button#button1");
        this.click("form button#button1");
      },
    function fail() {
        this.test.assertExists("form button#button1");
});

casper.run(function() {this.test.renderResults(true);});
```

Nevertheless, be careful; in some cases, we might need to manually modify the generated test because of the following reasons:

- ▸ It might contain a lot of useless assertions (due to extra clicks during the recording).

- ▸ It might be too heavy and verbose, making it more difficult to maintain. So, we would prefer to simplify it to focus on the most meaningful aspects.

- ▸ All assertions cannot be registered from Resurrectio, and we might need different assertions.

How it works...

One of the key advantages of CasperJS is its ability to chain test steps, knowing that these steps will be executed in the order they have been registered in.

As explained previously, the way to chain steps in JavaScript is by using callback functions as follows:

```
doStep1AndThen(function() {
    doStep2AndThen(function() {
        doStep3AndThen(function() {
            doStep4AndThen(function() {
                ...
            })
        })
    })
})
```

If we were using PhantomJS directly, that would be how our tests would look, and it would not be very convenient to read or maintain.

But with CasperJS, using the `then()` or `waitFor()` methods, we can declare successive steps without this infinite callback nesting cascade.

CasperJS does that callback chaining for us behind the scenes, creating much more readable test scripts.

There's more...

Let's see a few more details about the different features we have just used here.

XPath selectors

By default, CasperJS uses CSS3 selectors, but we can use XPath selectors if we prefer or if we have to.

XPath selectors are less readable than CSS3 selectors but they are more powerful (for instance, while matching text contents or putting conditions on the DOM element's ascendants or descendants).

To use XPath selectors, we just need to load the CasperJS `selectXPath` utility:

```
var x = require('casper').selectXPath;
...
    test.assertExists(x("//*[contains(text(), 'Barcelona
(Catalonia)')]"), 'The search results are correct');
```

Assertion methods

The CasperJS tester API offers a large collection of assertion methods.

We can assert conditions and function results in the following ways:

- The `assert(Boolean condition[, String message])` method asserts that the condition is strictly `true`

- The `assertNot(mixed subject[, String message])` method asserts that the condition is not `true`

- The `assertTruthy(Mixed subject[, String message])` method asserts that the subject is `truthy`

- The `assertFalsy(Mixed subject[, String message])` method asserts that the subject is `falsy`

Let's explain what `true`, `false`, `truthy`, and `falsy` is.

In JavaScript, `true` and `false` are the two Boolean values stricto sensu. Values such as `null`, `undefined`, the empty string `' '`, the number `0`, the number `NaN` are `falsy`, which means that if they are evaluated in a condition, they will return `false`.

And any other values are `truthy`, which means that if they are evaluated in a condition, they will return `true`.

- The `assertEquals(mixed testValue, mixed expected[, String message])` method asserts that the two parameters are equal

- The `assertNotEquals(mixed testValue, mixed expected[, String message])` method asserts that the two parameters are not equal

- The `assertEval(Function fn[, String message, Mixed arguments])` method asserts that the function evaluated in the page DOM returns `true`

  Example:

```
this.test.assertEval(function() {
    if(window.jQuery) {
        return true;
    } else {
```

```
        return false;
    }
}, "jQuery is available");
```

- The `assertEvalEquals(Function fn, mixed expected[, String message, Mixed arguments])` method asserts that the function evaluated in the DOM page returns the expected value

- The `assertMatch(mixed subject, RegExp pattern[, String message])` method asserts that the value matches the regular expression

- The `assertRaises(Function fn, Array args[, String message])` method asserts that the function called with the provided arguments raises an error

- The `assertType(mixed value, String type[, String message])` method asserts that the value type is the expected one

We can assert the DOM elements in the following ways:

- The `assertExists(String selector[, String message])` method asserts that the selector matches at least one element in the page

- The `assertDoesntExist(String selector[, String message])` method asserts that the selector does not match any element in the page

- The `assertField(String inputName, String expected[, String message])` method asserts that the form field has the expected value

- The `assertVisible(String selector[, String message])` method asserts that the element is visible

- The `assertNotVisible(String selector[, String message])` method asserts that the matched element is not visible

- The `assertSelectorHasText(String selector, String text[, String message])` method asserts that the matched element contains the expected text

- The `assertSelectorDoesntHaveText(String selector, String text[, String message])` method asserts that the matched element does not contain the given text

We can assert the page information in the following ways:

- The `assertHttpStatus(Number status[, String message])` method asserts that the current HTTP status is the expected one

- The `assertResourceExists(Function testFx[, String message])` method asserts that the resource exists on the page

 The parameter can be a string (the resource name), a regular expression (supposed to match at least one existing resource), or a function (supposed to return `true` for at least one of the existing resources).

- The `assertTextExists(String expected[, String message])` method asserts that the page contains the expected text

- The `assertTextDoesntExist(String unexpected[, String message])` method asserts that the page does not contain the given text

- The `assertTitle(String expected[, String message])` method asserts that the page title is the expected one

- The `assertTitleMatch(RegExp pattern[, String message])` method asserts that the page title matches the given regular expression

- The `assertUrlMatch(Regexp pattern[, String message])` method asserts that the page URL matches the given regular expression

The WaitFor methods

The following is the list of the CasperJS `waitFor` methods:

- The `waitForText(String|RegExp pattern[, Function then, Function onTimeout, Number timeout])` method waits until the text is present

- The `waitForSelector(String selector[, Function then, Function onTimeout, Number timeout])` method waits until the selector is satisfied

- The `waitWhileSelector(String selector[, Function then, Function onTimeout, Number timeout])` method waits until the selector is not satisfied anymore

- The `waitUntilVisible(String selector[, Function then, Function onTimeout, Number timeout])` method waits until the selected element is visible

- The `waitWhileVisible(String selector[, Function then, Function onTimeout, Number timeout])` method waits until the selected element is not visible anymore

- The `waitFor(Function testFx[, Function then, Function onTimeout, Number timeout])` method waits until the function returns true

- The `waitForResource(Function testFx[, Function then, Function onTimeout, Number timeout])` method waits until the function matches an existing resource

- The `waitForPopup(String|RegExp urlPattern[, Function then, Function onTimeout, Number timeout])` method waits until the pattern matches a pop-up URL

The wait() method

In the list of `waitFor` methods, we have not mentioned the following one:

```
wait(Number timeout[, Function then])
```

It just waits for a certain amount of time (in milliseconds).

But as discussed previously, in JavaScript, *time is nothing and timing is everything*. Similarly, in JavaScript, waiting for a given amount of time brings no guarantee to the accuracy of our test. Generally, we use `wait()` when we are desperate. For instance, if we have no way to modify the tested page, we cannot append an interesting signal to observe such as the `'noresult'` and `'success'` classes in our example.

Nevertheless, let's just note a relevant usage of the `wait()` method. When our page contains some progressive JPEG images and we want to capture a new image (see the *Beyond testing (Advanced)* recipe), we need to wait for some time before capturing, in order to let our images render entirely.

Installing Resurrectio from the GitHub sources

Resurrectio is not entirely stable yet, so it might be interesting to use the current development version.

To do so, you have to clone the `resurrectio` GitHub repository:

```
~ git clone git://github.com/ebrehault/resurrectio.git
```

It will produce a `./resurrectio` folder.

Then, in Chrome, perform the following steps:

1. Go to **Tools | Extensions**.
2. Check the **Developer mode** checkbox.
3. Click on the **Load unpacked extension** button.
4. Select the `./resurrectio` folder.

Writing advanced tests (Intermediate)

This recipe will detail how to simulate rich web interactions using CasperJS, in order to achieve more complex testing.

How to do it...

The following sections cover the various steps in writing advanced tests.

Downloading files

First, let's learn how to download files. The most common way to download a file from a web page is by providing a link to this file as follows (`example4.html`):

```html
<html><body>
    <h1>My example</h1>
    <a id="link-to-text" href="files/text.txt">Download a text</a>
    <a id="link-to-pdf" href="files/text.pdf">Download a PDF</a>
</body></html>
```

Now, let's create the following CasperJS script (`example4.js`):

```javascript
var casper = require('casper').create();

casper.start('http://localhost:8000/example4.html', function() {
    this.click("#link-to-text");
});
casper.then(function() {
    this.echo(this.getCurrentUrl());
});

casper.thenOpen('http://localhost:8000/example4.html', function() {
    this.click("#link-to-pdf");
});

casper.then(function() {
    this.echo(this.getCurrentUrl());
});

casper.run();
```

It should open our page, click on the first link, log the current page URL, reopen the page, click on the second link, and log the current page URL.

To complete our test, let's create a folder named `files`, add two dummy files in this folder (`text.txt` and `text.pdf`), and start our SimpleHTTPServer web server.

Let's run the script:

```
~ casperjs example4.js
http://localhost:8000/files/text.txt
http://localhost:8000/example4.html
~ ls
example4.html   example4.js   files
~
```

When we clicked on the first link, we actually opened the `.txt` file as a page, but when we clicked on the second one, we opened the file that was kept in the original location. If we check the current folder content, we will see that nothing has been downloaded.

So the `click()` method will not help us in downloading any file; it will navigate to the corresponding link if PhantomJS is able to open it, or it will open the file that was kept in the original location, producing no error and no output.

The right way to download a file is by using the `download()` method. Let's fix our test using the following code:

```
var casper = require('casper').create();
casper.start('http://localhost:8000/example4.html', function() {
    this.download("http://localhost:8000/files/text.txt", "text.txt");
    this.download("http://localhost:8000/files/text.pdf", "text.pdf");
});


casper.run();
```

The outcome looks as follows:

```
~ casperjs example4.js
~ ls
example4.html  example4.js  files  text.pdf  text.txt
~ 
```

Now that our files have been downloaded, let's discover how to upload files.

Uploading files

To perform a file upload during a test, we will use the `fill()` method. The `fill()` method allows us to fill in a form and optionally, to submit it. Plus, it is able to manage file inputs.

The following is an example (`example5.js`):

```
var x = require('casper').selectXPath;
casper.test.begin('Upload a file', 1, function(test) {
    casper.start('http://imagebin.org/', function() {
        this.click(x("//a[normalize-space(text())='Add your image
now!']"));
    });

    casper.then(function() {
        this.fill("form[name=image_form]", {
            'nickname' : 'casper',
            'image': './test.png',
            'title': 'my test',
            'description': 'just a test',
```

```
                    'disclaimer_agree': 'Y'
            }, true);
        });

    casper.then(function() {
            test.assertExists('img[alt="my test"]', "The image has been
    uploaded");
            this.echo("It is available here: " + this.getCurrentUrl());
        });

    casper.run(function() {
            test.done();
        });
    });
```

You can perform the following steps with this test:

1. Go to `http://imagebin.org`.
2. Click on the **Add your image now!** link.
3. Then, fill in the image submission form.
4. Assert that we obtain a page containing our image.
5. Display this page URL.

As we can see, the `'image'` field is managed the same way as the other fields; its value is just the path to our local image.

After passing the first parameter containing the fields values, we pass `true` as a second parameter to `fill()`, so that the form is submitted.

Before running the test, we make sure that we put an image named `test.png` in our current folder and when we run the test, the following is what we get:

```
~ casperjs test example5.js
Test file: example5.js
# Upload a file
PASS The image has been uploaded
It is available here: http://imagebin.org/273748
PASS 1 test executed in 4.024s, 1 passed, 0 failed, 0 dubious, 0 skipped.
~
```

Authentication

Let's see how we can manage authentication. When we try to open a page that requires authentication, we get a 401 HTTP error (`example6.js`):

```
casper.test.begin('Log in', 1, function(test) {
    casper.start('http://www.plomino.net/zmiroot/testpage', function()
    {
```

```
        test.assertHttpStatus(401, 'We cannot see the page as we are
not logged in.');
    });

    casper.run(function() {
        test.done();
    });
});
```

The outcome is as follows:

```
~ casperjs test example6.js
Test file: example6.js
# Log in
PASS We cannot see the page as we are not logged in.
PASS 1 test executed in 0.26s, 1 passed, 0 failed, 0 dubious, 0 skipped.
~
```

Now, let's use the `setHttpAuth()` method to log in properly:

```
casper.test.begin('Log in', 1, function(test) {
    casper.start();

    casper.setHttpAuth('demoaccount', 'demoaccount');

    casper.thenOpen('http://www.plomino.net/zmiroot/testpage',
function() {
        test.assertTextExists('You are logged in.', 'Now we can see
the page.');
    });
    casper.run(function() {
        test.done();
    });
});
```

The following is what we get:

```
~ casperjs test example6.js
Test file: example6.js
# Log in
PASS Now we can see the page.
PASS 1 test executed in 0.269s, 1 passed, 0 failed, 0 dubious, 0 skipped.
~
```

The `setHttpAuth()` method can only be used for HTTP authentication. When our targeted page uses a web form authentication, we just need to fill the authentication form. The following is an example (`example7.js`):

```
casper.test.begin('Log in', 1, function(test) {
    casper.start('http://www.plomino.net/samples', function() {
        this.fill('#loginform',
            {
                '__ac_name': 'demouser',
                '__ac_password': 'demouser'
            }, true);
    });

    casper.then(function() {
        test.assertTextExists('Welcome! You are now logged in', 'We
are logged in.');
    });

    casper.run(function() {
        test.done();
    });
});
```

The output looks as follows:

Keyboard and mouse events

Simulating keyboard and mouse events is another very common use case. Let's consider the following page (example8.html):

```
<html><body>
    <script>
    function updateMessage(element) {
        var message = 'You have entered ' + element.value.length + '
characters.';
        document.querySelector('#message').textContent = message;
    }
    </script>
    <h1>My example</h1>
    <form id="my-form">
        <p>Firstname: <input
            type="text"
            name="firstname"
            onkeyup="updateMessage(this);"/>
        </p>
        <div id="message"></div>
    </form>
</body></html>
```

If we launch our simple HTTP server, we can try opening the page at `http://localhost:8000/example8.html`.

When we enter a value in the input text, a message is displayed under the input text, indicating the number of characters we have entered.

To test this behavior, we can use the `sendKeys()` method (`example8.js`):

```javascript
casper.test.begin('Test key inputs', 1, function(test) {
    casper.start('http://localhost:8000/example8.html', function() {
        this.sendKeys('input[name="firstname"]', 'Eric');
    });
    casper.then(function() {
        test.assertSelectorHasText('#message', "You have entered 4
characters.");
    });
    casper.run(function() {
        test.done();
    });
});
```

When we run the code, we will see the following result. If you enter `Eric` in the text input, the message will display **You have entered 4 characters**:

```
~ casperjs test example8.js
Test file: example8.js
# Test key inputs
PASS Found "You have entered 4 characters." within the selector "#message"
PASS 1 test executed in 0.096s, 1 passed, 0 failed, 0 dubious, 0 skipped.
~
```

The `sendKeys()` method inserted the text into the text input and also triggered the `onkeyup` event.

The `sendKeys()` method can produce a key event on any element of the page (not necessarily inputs).

Let's change the page `example8.html` so that the header becomes editable:

```html
<h1 contenteditable="true">My example</h1>
```

Now if we click on the header, we can change its text content.

Let's modify our test script:

```javascript
casper.test.begin('Test key inputs', 2, function(test) {
    casper.start('http://localhost:8000/example8.html', function() {
        this.sendKeys('input[name="firstname"]', 'Eric');
    });
    casper.then(function() {
```

```
    test.assertSelectorHasText('#message', "You have entered 4
characters.");
    });
    casper.then(function() {
        this.click('h1');
        this.sendKeys('h1', 'I have changed my header');
    });
    casper.then(function() {
        test.assertSelectorHasText('h1', "I have changed my header");
    });
    casper.run(function() {
        test.done();
    });
});
```

Now, perform the following steps with this test:

- Click on the header and enter a new text at its beginning
- Assert the new header content

The output will be as follows:

```
~ casperjs test example8.js
Test file: example8.js
# Test key inputs
PASS Found "You have entered 4 characters." within the selector "#message"
PASS Found "I have changed my header" within the selector "h1"
PASS 2 tests executed in 0.138s, 2 passed, 0 failed, 0 dubious, 0 skipped.
~
```

As we have an extra assertion in our test script now, we have changed the `begin()` method's second parameter from 1 to 2.

Regarding mouse events, we have already used the `casper.click()` method. It takes a selector as a parameter and triggers a click event on the designated element.

We use it to click on links or buttons, for instance.

We can also trigger other mouse events using the `mouseEvent()` method; its first parameter is the event type and the second is the targeted element selector.

It can trigger the following events:

- `mouseup`
- `mousedown`
- `click`

- mousemove

- mouseover

- mouseout

Let's create the following web page (`example9.html`):

```html
<html><body>
    <h1 id="chap1">Chapter 1</h1>
    <h1 id="chap2">Chapter 2</h1>
    <h1 id="chap3">Chapter 3</h1>
    <h1 id="chap4">Chapter 4</h1>
    <div>Counter: <span id="counter"></span></div>
    <script>
var counter = 0;
function incrementCounter() {
    counter =  counter + 1;
    document.querySelector('#counter').textContent = counter;
}
for(i=0;i<document.querySelectorAll("h1").length;i++) {
    document.querySelectorAll("h1")[i].onmouseover=incrementCounter;
}
    </script>
</body></html>
```

It presents a list of headers and when the mouse goes over any of them, a counter is incremented.

We can test this page using `mouseEvent ()`, as shown in the following test (`example9.js`):

```javascript
casper.test.begin('Test mouse events', 1, function(test) {
    casper.start('http://localhost:8000/example9.html', function() {
        this.mouseEvent('mouseover', '#chap1');
        this.mouseEvent('mouseover', '#chap4');
        this.mouseEvent('mouseover', '#chap1');
        this.mouseEvent('mouseover', '#chap1');
    });
    casper.then(function() {
        test.assertSelectorHasText('#counter', "4");
    });

    casper.run(function() {
        test.done();
     });

});
```

The outcome is as follows:

```
~ casperjs test example9.js
Test file: example9.js
# Test mouse events
PASS Found "4" within the selector "#counter"
PASS 1 test executed in 0.116s, 1 passed, 0 failed, 0 dubious, 0 skipped.
~
```

But CasperJS also provides a specific `'mouse'` module to control the mouse directly. It allows to move the mouse and to control the click (down, up, click, double-click).

It might be useful if we want to test complex mouse interaction such as drag-and-drop. The following is a web page that provides a draggable box (`example10.html`) using the jQueryUI `draggable()` method:

```html
<html>
<head>
<style>
#box {color: white; background-color: blue; width: 100px; position:
absolute; top: 0; left: 0;}
</style>
</head>
<body>
    <script src="http://code.jquery.com/jquery-1.9.1.js"></script>
    <script src="http://code.jquery.com/ui/1.10.3/jquery-ui.js"></
script>
    <script>
$(document).ready(function() {
    $('#box').draggable();
});
    </script>
    <div id="box">My box</div>
</body></html>
```

We can test this page using the CasperJS mouse module (`example10.js`):

```javascript
casper.options.viewportSize = {width: 1024, height: 768};

casper.test.begin('Test drag&drop', 2, function(test) {
    casper.start('http://localhost:8000/example10.html', function() {
        test.assertEval(function() {
            var pos = $('#box').position();
            return (pos.left == 0 && pos.top == 0);
        }, "The box is at the top");
        this.mouse.down(5, 5);
        this.mouse.move(400, 200);
```

```
            this.mouse.up(400, 200);
        });
        casper.then(function() {
            test.assertEval(function() {
                var pos = $('#box').position();
                return (pos.left == 395 && pos.top == 195);
            }, "The box has been moved");
        });
        casper.run(function() {
            test.done();
        });
    });
```

The output will be as follows:

```
~ casperjs test example10.js
Test file: example10.js
# Test drag&drop
PASS The box is at the top
PASS The box has been moved
PASS 2 tests executed in 1.133s, 2 passed, 0 failed, 0 dubious, 0 skipped.
~
```

We can see that there are a lot of interesting things in this test:

- We set the viewport size (using the `viewportSize` option). In our case, it is useful because we need to make sure that we have enough room to move the box where we want.

- We use jQuery to get the current position of the box! As jQuery is loaded in our tested page, we can use it through `assertEval()`, as *it runs the code in the tested page*.

- We use `down()`, then `move()`, and then `up()` to produce a drag-and-drop move from point (5,5) to point (400,200).

How it works...

Even if they might seem quite similar, there are differences between `casper.click()` and `casper.mouse.click()`.

First of all, `casper.click()` only accepts a selector as a parameter, while `casper.mouse.click()` accepts either a selector or a (x, y) position.

But more importantly, they do not work the same way; `casper.click()` creates an event and *dispatches* it to the targeted event, but `casper.mouse.click()` does not deal with any element and just *produces a mouse action* at the given position.

If `casper.click()` is not able to dispatch the event (because of a `preventDefault()` method hanging somewhere), it will default to the `casper.mouse.click()` method.

casper.mouseEvent() works exactly as casper.click().

There's more...

Let's explore a few more details about the different features we have just used in the previous section.

Passing parameters to the download() method

The download() method might also accept two extra parameters as follows:

```
download(String url, String target[, String method, Object data])
```

So, we can produce an HTTP request using the method we want and pass the needed arguments in the data object.

setHttpAuth might have surprising timing

Consider that we come back to our test (example6.js) about setHttpAuth() and try to chain the two versions as follows:

```
casper.test.begin('Log in', 2, function(test) {

    casper.start('http://www.plomino.net/zmiroot/testpage', function()
{
        test.assertHttpStatus(401, 'We cannot see the page as we are
not logged in.');
    });

    casper.setHttpAuth('demoaccount', 'demoaccount');

    casper.thenOpen('http://www.plomino.net/zmiroot/testpage',
function() {
        test.assertTextExists('You are logged in.', 'Now we can see
the page.');
    });
    casper.run(function() {
        test.done();
    });
});
```

We would expect the tests to be successful due to the following conditions: we get a 401 error if we are anonymous and are able to view the page if we log in.

But, the following is what we obtain:

```
~ casperjs test example6.js
Test file: example6.js
# Log in
FAIL We cannot see the page as we are not logged in.
#    type: assertHttpStatus
#    file: example6.js:4
#    code: test.assertHttpStatus(401, 'We cannot see the page as we are not logg
ed in.');
#    subject: false
#    current: 200
#    expected: 401
PASS Now we can see the page.
FAIL 2 tests executed in 0.334s, 1 passed, 1 failed, 0 dubious, 0 skipped.

Details for the 1 failed test:

In example6.js:4
  Log in
    assertHttpStatus: We cannot see the page as we are not logged in.
~ 
```

The first test fails; we do not get a 401 error, but we get a 200 status instead! This means we are actually logged in.

Why is that? It's because CasperJS chains the steps that are enclosed into `then()` blocks. If `setHttpAuth()` is not enclosed in a `then()` block, it will be effective right from the beginning (the `start()` call) to the end.

Let's enclose it in a `then()` block as follows:

```javascript
casper.test.begin('Log in', 2, function(test) {

    casper.start('http://www.plomino.net/zmiroot/testpage', function()
    {
        test.assertHttpStatus(401, 'We cannot see the page as we are
    not logged in.');
    });

    casper.then(function() {
        this.setHttpAuth('demoaccount', 'demoaccount');
    })

    casper.thenOpen('http://www.plomino.net/zmiroot/testpage',
    function() {
        test.assertTextExists('You are logged in.', 'Now we can see
    the page.');
    });
```

```
    casper.run(function() {
        test.done();
    });
});
```

And now, the tests pass as follows:

```
~ casperjs test example6.js
Test file: example6.js
# Log in
PASS We cannot see the page as we are not logged in.
PASS Now we can see the page.
PASS 2 tests executed in 0.423s, 2 passed, 0 failed, 0 dubious, 0 skipped.
~
```

Best practices (Intermediate)

This section will discuss the essential best practices for web functional testing with CasperJS.

Testing the real thing

Our software quality depends on our tests' accuracy. Testing is always good, but if we don't test the software's behavior accurately, we might miss out on some potential problems. To create accurate tests, we must forget about the system and how it works, and we must focus on user interactions.

It might sound obvious but it is not, because most of the time we design and code the system and do not use it (as a standard user) a lot.

Let's consider a typical example of a basic web form. Here is an important thing to know about web forms: *users never submit web forms*. They actually do the following:

▶ Enter values into inputs

▶ Click on the **Submit** button

These actions do produce a form submission, but the users don't actually submit the form by themselves; their web browsers do it for them. Or, let's say the system does it for them.

Obviously, if we want to test this system, we cannot rely on its supposed behavior.

That is why our tests must produce the real user interactions and then assert that the resulting behavior is correct.

Let's have a look at the following example (`example11.html`):

```html
<html><body>
  <form id="form1">
```

```html
      <p>Firstname: <input type="text" name="firstname"/></p>
      <p>Lastname: <input type="text" name="lastname"/></p>
      <p>Age: <input type="text" name="age"/></p>
      <input type="submit" value="Save" name="save" />
    </form>
    <form id="form2">
      <p>Firstname: <input type="text" name="firstname"/></p>
      <p>Lastname: <input type="text" name="lastname"/></p>
       <p>Age: <input type="text" name="age"/></p>
    </form>
    <form id="form3">
      <p>Firstname: <input type="text" name="firstname"/></p>
      <p>Lastname: <input type="text" name="lastname"/></p>
      <p>Age: <input style="display: none;" type="text" name="age"/></p>
      <input type="submit" value="Save" name="save" />
    </form>
  </body></html>
```

This page shows the following three forms:

- The first one contains first name, last name, and age, and a **Save** button
- The second one has the same fields but no **Save** button
- The third one has all the fields and a **Save** button, but the age field is hidden

If we launch our simple HTTP server, the first one will work fine, but the other two will not be usable.

Now, let's test it as follows (`example11-1.js`):

```javascript
var formid = casper.cli.options['formid'];

casper.test.begin('Test form submission', 3, function(test) {

    casper.start('http://localhost:8000/example11.html', function() {
        this.fill("#" + formid, {
            firstname: "Isaac",
            lastname: "Newton",
            age: "370",
        }, true);
    });
    casper.then(function() {
        test.assertUrlMatch(/firstname=Isaac/);
        test.assertUrlMatch(/lastname=Newton/);
        test.assertUrlMatch(/age=370/);
    });
```

```
casper.run(function() {
    test.done();
});
});
```

This test uses `casper.fill()` to submit the form with a value for each field and then asserts so we obtain the three values in the resulting URL.

In this test, we use `casper.cli.options` to read options passed to the `casperjs` command; this way, we can use the same script to test the three different forms.

Let's run it. The following screenshot shows the output:

```
~ casperjs test example11-1.js --formid=form1
Test file: example11-1.js
# Test form submission
PASS Current url matches the provided pattern
PASS Current url matches the provided pattern
PASS Current url matches the provided pattern
PASS 3 tests executed in 0.094s, 3 passed, 0 failed, 0 dubious, 0 skipped.
~ casperjs test example11-1.js --formid=form2
Test file: example11-1.js
# Test form submission
PASS Current url matches the provided pattern
PASS Current url matches the provided pattern
PASS Current url matches the provided pattern
PASS 3 tests executed in 0.128s, 3 passed, 0 failed, 0 dubious, 0 skipped.
~ casperjs test example11-1.js --formid=form3
Test file: example11-1.js
# Test form submission
PASS Current url matches the provided pattern
PASS Current url matches the provided pattern
PASS Current url matches the provided pattern
PASS 3 tests executed in 0.105s, 3 passed, 0 failed, 0 dubious, 0 skipped.
~
```

The tests pass with the first form as expected, but they also pass with the other two!

Why is that? It's because the `fill()` method is blind to the mistakes we have introduced in the forms; it just performs a submission without checking if a real user could actually do the same.

The following is a test that is closer to real user interaction (`example11-2.js`):

```
var formid = casper.cli.options['formid'];

casper.test.begin('Test form submission', 3, function(test) {
    casper.start('http://localhost:8000/example11.html', function() {
        this.sendKeys("form#"+formid+" input[name='firstname']",
"Isaac");
```

```
        this.sendKeys("form#"+formid+" input[name='lastname']",
"Newton");
        this.sendKeys("form#"+formid+" input[name='age']", "370");
        this.click("form#"+formid+" input[type=submit]
[value='Save']");
    });
    casper.then(function() {
        test.assertUrlMatch(/firstname=Isaac/);
        test.assertUrlMatch(/lastname=Newton/);
        test.assertUrlMatch(/age=370/);
    });

    casper.run(function() {
        test.done();
    });
});
```

Here we use `sendKeys()` to enter the values in the inputs, and we use the `click()` method to click on the **Submit** button. This is basically what the user would do with his or her keyboard and mouse.

Now let's run it. The following screenshot shows the output:

```
~ casperjs test example11-2.js --formid=form1
Test file: example11-2.js
# Test form submission
PASS Current url matches the provided pattern
PASS Current url matches the provided pattern
PASS Current url matches the provided pattern
PASS 3 tests executed in 0.103s, 3 passed, 0 failed, 0 dubious, 0 skipped.
~ casperjs test example11-2.js --formid=form2
Test file: example11-2.js
# Test form submission
FAIL Cannot dispatch mousedown event on nonexistent selector: form#form2 input[t
ype=submit][value='Save']
#     type: uncaughtError
#     file: example11-2.js:1323
#     error: Cannot dispatch mousedown event on nonexistent selector: form#form2
input[type=submit][value='Save']
#           CasperError: Cannot dispatch mousedown event on nonexistent selector
: form#form2 input[type=submit][value='Save']
#               at mouseEvent (/home/ebr/bin/casperjs/modules/casper.js:1323)
#               at click (/home/ebr/bin/casperjs/modules/casper.js:428)
#               at example11-2.js:8
#               at runStep (/home/ebr/bin/casperjs/modules/casper.js:1523)
#               at checkStep (/home/ebr/bin/casperjs/modules/casper.js:368)
#     stack: not provided
FAIL Current url matches the provided pattern
#     type: assertUrlMatch
#     file: example11-2.js:11
#     code: test.assertUrlMatch(/firstname=Isaac/);
#     subject: false
#     currentUrl: "http://localhost:8000/example11.html"
#     pattern: "/firstname=Isaac/"
FAIL 2 tests executed in 0.099s, 0 passed, 2 failed, 0 dubious, 0 skipped.

Details for the 2 failed tests:

In example11-2.js:1323
  Test form submission
    uncaughtError: Cannot dispatch mousedown event on nonexistent selector: form
#form2 input[type=submit][value='Save']
In example11-2.js:11
  Test form submission
    assertUrlMatch: Current url matches the provided pattern
~ casperjs test example11-2.js --formid=form3
Test file: example11-2.js
# Test form submission
PASS Current url matches the provided pattern
PASS Current url matches the provided pattern
FAIL Current url matches the provided pattern
#     type: assertUrlMatch
#     file: example11-2.js:13
#     code: test.assertUrlMatch(/age=370/);
#     subject: false
#     currentUrl: "http://localhost:8000/example11.html?firstname=Isaac&lastname=
Newton&age=&save=Save"
#     pattern: "/age=370/"
FAIL 3 tests executed in 0.108s, 2 passed, 1 failed, 0 dubious, 0 skipped.

Details for the 1 failed test:

In example11-2.js:13
  Test form submission
    assertUrlMatch: Current url matches the provided pattern
~
```

This is much better; now our tests fail at the second and third forms.

This does not mean that we must never use the `fill()` method. That was just an example. The main point here is that we must always be careful to keep as close as possible to the user interactions. But of course, we also need to create concise and maintainable tests.

So a good approach is to write several kinds of tests, such as the following:

- Some precise tests focusing on the user interactions (where we will use `sendKeys()` and `click()` instead of `fill()`, for instance) to make sure each page is usable by itself
- Some concise tests focusing on screen chaining and usage scenarios (where we can use `fill()`, for instance) to make sure the complete application is working fine

Surviving design changes

Some people prefer to write tests at the end of their development, when they know everything is pretty much stable.

But the best time to write tests is from the beginning to the end of the development. This has already been demonstrated in a lot of books, but one of the most obvious reasons is that we usually produce the biggest part of our bugs during the development phase, and tests are a great help to fight bugs.

Unfortunately, people who write tests at the end are right: the website is (usually) more stable after development than during development.

One of the aspects that might change a lot is the design. Design changes should not impact application features. But sometimes they do, and there may be a lot of reasons for it, such as a CSS attribute can make a button invisible, modification in an element's ID can break a JavaScript call, and so on. But we do not mind this much, because if the design breaks any feature, our tests will warn us immediately.

The problem is that sometimes our tests fail even if the design changes haven't broken any features. This is very bad because it implies that we cannot trust our tests to know whether something is broken or not.

Why our tests would fail if all the features have been preserved? This is just because our tests are less design-proof than our web page features, and the writing of design-proof tests depends mainly on selectors.

Indeed, our test inner logic (for example, if we click *here*, we should get *that*) should not be impacted by design changes.

But what could easily break if we are not careful enough is the way we define *here* and *that*. They will be defined using selectors. We must choose selectors that focus on the logic and not on the layout.

The following are some examples:

Instead of	Prefer	Because
`"div#form-container span input"`	`"form[name='registration'] input[name='firstname']"`	We only depend on form elements and their names
`"div ul li:first-child a"`	`"#results .result:first-child a"`	We use IDs and classes instead of tag names
`"a#reset-btn"`	`x("//a[normalize-space(text())='Reset']")`	We use the link text instead of its ID (and to do this, we switch to the XPath selector)

By doing this, we can change our design, switch from Bootstrap to Foundation, reorganize the layout, and so on, and be sure that if the tests fail, they do for a good reason: because we have actually broken the logic.

Creating test suites

Until now, we have created single test scripts for our different example pages, but when we test our real applications, we will need to test a lot of different features and scenarios.

It will definitely work if we do it in a single long test script, but obviously, it will be more difficult to refactor it, maintain it, share it with a team, and so on.

So, quite a simple, good practice is to split our different feature tests and testing scenarios into separate scripts. And fortunately, CasperJS provides the `casperjs test` command so we can run all our tests at once.

Let's reuse our `example8.html` page from the previous chapter. This page proposes two features: an editable header and a simple form with text input.

Let's imagine that we want to create two different tests for these two features. So let's create a folder (named `suit`, for instance), and in this folder, create the files `test_editable_header.js` and `test_form.js`.

Create `test_editable_header.js` as follows:

```
casper.test.begin('Test editable header', 1, function(test) {
  casper.start('http://localhost:8000/example8.html', function() {
    this.click('h1');
    this.sendKeys('h1', 'I have changed ');
  });
  casper.then(function() {
```

```
      test.assertSelectorHasText('h1', "I have changed my header");
    });
    casper.run(function() {
      test.done();
    });
  });
```

Create `test_form.js` js as follows:

```
casper.test.begin('Test editable header', 1, function(test) {
  casper.start('http://localhost:8000/example8.html', function() {
    this.sendKeys('input[name="firstname"]', 'Eric');
  });
  casper.then(function() {
    test.assertSelectorHasText('#message', "You have entered 4
characters.");
  });

  casper.run(function() {
    test.done();
  });
});
```

And now, let's launch our tests:

```
~ casperjs test ./suite
Test file: /home/ebr/tmp/chap3/suite/test_editable_header.js
# Test editable header
PASS Found "I have changed my header" within the selector "h1"
Test file: /home/ebr/tmp/chap3/suite/test_form.js
# Test editable header
PASS Found "You have entered 4 characters." within the selector "#message"
PASS 2 tests executed in 0.199s, 2 passed, 0 failed, 0 dubious, 0 skipped.
~
```

As we can see in the preceding screenshot, we have passed our folder path to the `casperjs test` command, and it has run all the tests contained in this folder.

The `casperjs test` command offers interesting options, as follows:

- `--fail-fast`: This is used to stop the test suite at the *first error*
- `--pre=pre-test.js`: This is used to run a test *before* executing the test suite
- `--post=post-test.js`: This is used to run a test *after* executing the test suite
- `--includes=file1.js,file2.js`: This is used to include some tests *before* running *each test* in the suite
- `--direct`: This is used to output the log message in the console

- `--log-level=<level>`: This is used to choose the log level (DEBUG, INFO, WARNING, or ERROR)
- `--xunit=<filename>`: This is used to export the test results to the xUnit format

The `--pre` and `--post` options are typically used to implement a pre-test setup and post-test tear down, respectively.

For instance, if our system allows users to modify their preferences and we want to test it, the pre-test setup will create a fake user profile so we can test profile preference change. The post-test tear down will remove this fake user profile, so the next time we run the test suite, it will not break because the profile already exists.

Running CasperJS on Jenkins

Writing tests is a good starting point, but then we have to make sure we run them often enough. One of the **Continuous Integration** (**CI**) principles is to run the tests each time we commit a change in the source repository. To do this, we need a CI tool, and Jenkins is one of the most widely used ones.

We will not cover the detailed Jenkins installation and configuration here as it is not a desktop application but a service exposed by a server. We assume it is deployed on one of our servers.

To run our CasperJS tests on Jenkins, we need first to make sure that PhantomJS and CasperJS are installed on the machine where Jenkins is running (refer to the *Installing CasperJS* section).

Then, we open the Jenkins web interface and click on **New Job** as shown in the following screenshot:

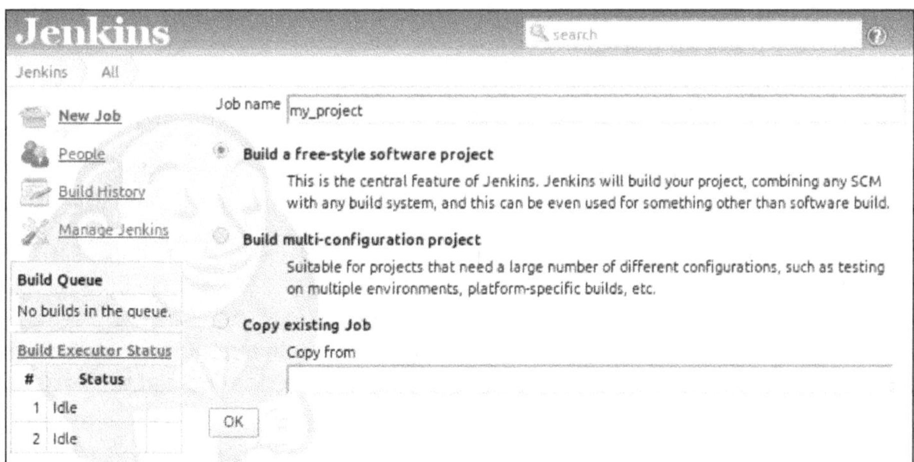

In the **Build** section, we add a new **Execute shell** step:

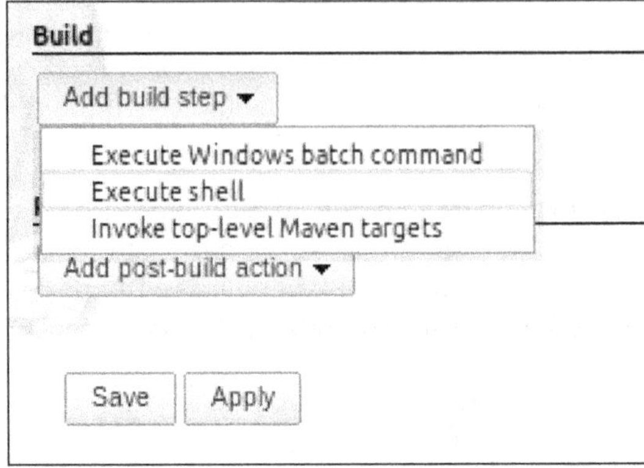

Then we click on **Save** and enter our test command in the **Build** section.

Assuming our tests are in a folder named `tests` at the root of our repository, we would enter the following:

```
casperjs test ./tests
```

The following screenshot shows the textbox in which we will add the preceding command:

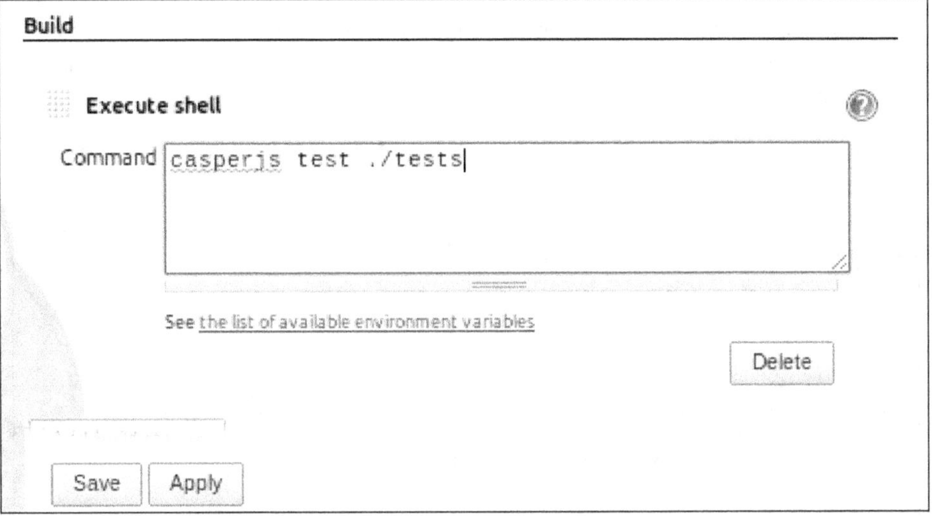

We can now launch a build manually or let Jenkins launch builds automatically (depending on the triggers we have chosen). Jenkins will directly interpret the CasperJS output, and we will get a build history showing failures and successes as follows:

We can also see the details of a given build as in the following screenshot:

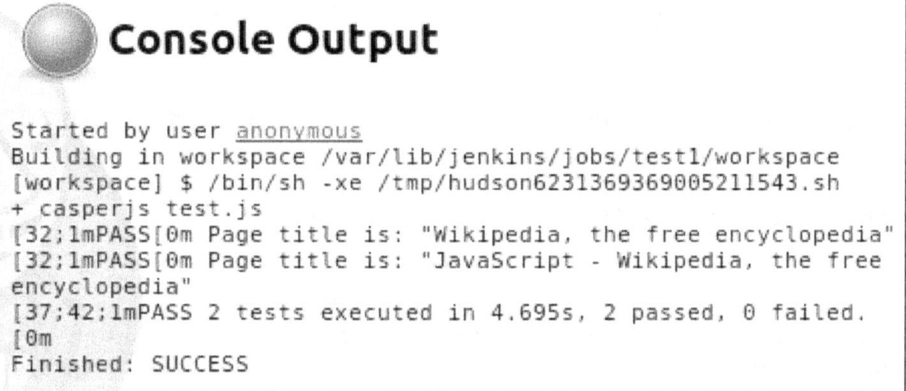

Running CasperJS on Travis-CI

Travis-CI is a Cloud service that can be hooked to our GitHub repositories. It is free for public repositories. Each time we push changes to GitHub, Travis-CI does the following:

- Creates a blank virtual machine
- Checks the current sources from GitHub
- Deploys our application
- Runs the tests
- Notifies the user (via e-mail, IRC, and so on)

It also does the same when we receive a pull request on our GitHub repository so we know whether the submitted pull request breaks the tests or not before merging it. This information is displayed directly on GitHub.

To run CasperJS tests on Travis-CI, we need to do the following:

1. Go to `travis-ci.org` and sign in with our GitHub account.
2. Go to **Profile** and copy the token.
3. Go to the GitHub repository, click on **Settings / Service Hooks**, choose **Travis-CI**, enter our GitHub ID and the previously copied Travis token, check **Active**, and click on **Update**.
4. Add a `.travis.yml` file in the root of our repository.

This `.travis.yml` file is used to explain to Travis how to deploy the test environment and how to run the tests.

We just need to deploy CasperJS because PhantomJS is preinstalled on Travis.

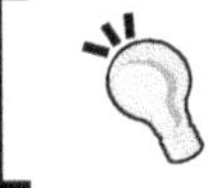

Since PhantomJS is completely headless, there is no need run Xvfb.

The following is a typical `.travis.yml` file:

```
install:
  - git clone git://github.com/n1k0/casperjs.git
  - cd casperjs; git checkout tags/1.1; cd -
before_script:
  - "export PHANTOMJS_EXECUTABLE='phantomjs --local-to-remote-url-
access=yes --ignore-ssl-errors=yes'"
script:
  - ./casperjs/bin/casperjs test ./tests
```

In the `install` section, we download the CasperJS code and check the last stable version. In the `before_script` section, we set up PhantomJS to allow access to external URLs, and in the `script` section, we launch the tests.

Just like Jenkins, Travis-CI will interpret the CasperJS output result as a success or failure, and we will be notified accordingly. Our tests can target a local server, and if so, our `.travis.yml` file will need to deploy the needed HTTP server and its components.

But the tests can also target an external URL, and if so, we have to make sure the code is updated on the real server as soon as it is pushed to GitHub. This can be done conveniently using GitHub pages.

Beyond testing (Advanced)

This section will present other CasperJS usages apart from testing.

Web scripting

Web scripting means to run a script that will use web pages as a backend service.

Of course, scripting a web page is quite a brutal way to obtain a service. Using a REST API (or any API) would be much more elegant. But in some cases there is no API. CasperJS is able to simulate user interaction on our web pages in order to test them.

But obviously, we can use its abilities to simulate user interaction on any web page in order to automate a process. That is why CasperJS is a very efficient web scripting tool.

Let's say we want a script to tell us how many unread messages we have in our Gmail inbox. We could use a script like the following (`example12.js`):

```
var casper = require('casper').create();

casper.userAgent('Mozilla/5.0 (Macintosh; Intel Mac OS X)');
casper.start("http://mail.google.com");

casper.waitForSelector("form#gaia_loginform", function() {
  this.sendKeys('form#gaia_loginform input[name="Email"]', "<my_
account>@gmail.com");
  this.sendKeys('form#gaia_loginform input[name="Passwd"]',
"<password>");
});

casper.then(function() {
    this.click("#signIn");
});

casper.then(function() {
    var inbox_link_text = this.fetchText('table.m a[accesskey="i"]');


    var search_unread = /\(((\d+)\)/.exec(inbox_link_text );
    if(!search_unread) {
        this.echo("No new emails.", 'INFO');
    } else {
        this.echo("You have " + search_unread[1] + " new emails.",
'INFO');
    }
});

casper.run();
```

In this script, we log in and get the HTML code for the **Inbox** link (in the left menu) as it contains the number of unread e-mails, like the following:

```
Inbox (53)
```

To extract the number, we use a regular expression, $/\((\d+)\)/$, that will look for any number enclosed in brackets.

And the following is what we get:

```
~ casperjs example12.js
You have 53 new emails.
~
```

Now let's try to get a local weather report (`example13.js`):

```javascript
var casper = require('casper').create();

casper.start("http://weather.yahoo.com/");

casper.then(function() {
    var current_location = this.fetchText('#location-chooser .name');
    var current_temp = this.fetchText('.temp .f .num');
    this.echo("Current temperature in " + current_location + ": " +
current_temp + "°F");
});
casper.run();
```

Here, we just load the Yahoo! Weather home page and then extract the information we want (the current temperature, our location, and the immediate forecast). After we have done this, we get the following:

```
~ casperjs example13.js
Current temperature in Upper Garonne: 64°F
~
```

Nice!

But be careful; if Yahoo! decides to change its weather page's layout, the selectors we have used might become invalid and our service would be down. This is the main weakness of the web scripting approach. And, in this very use case (getting Yahoo! Weather reports), we will build a much safer service by using the excellent Yahoo! Query Language REST API.

Nevertheless, web scripting might sometimes be a light and convenient solution when we are facing complex cross-platform integration issues.

Screenshot production

CasperJS is able to produce an image from the current page using the following two methods:

- `this.capture(String filepath)`: This takes a screenshot of the entire page
- `this.captureSelector(String filepath, String selector)`: This restricts the capture to a specific element

A simple example (`example14.js`) is as follows:

```
var casper = require('casper').create();

casper.start('http://en.wikipedia.org/wiki/Solar_System');

casper.then(function() {
    this.capture("screenshot1.png");
});

casper.run();
```

If we run it, it'll work just fine, but we will obtain a very large image because this Wikipedia page is very long and we have captured it entirely.

Being able to obtain a screenshot of a very long page is not always easy, so this feature can be helpful. If we want to reduce the captured area, we can set the viewport size and use `captureSelector` on the `html` element as follows:

```
var casper = require('casper').create();

casper.options.viewportSize = {width: 1300, height: 700};
casper.start('http://en.wikipedia.org/wiki/Solar_System');

casper.then(function() {
    this.captureSelector("screenshot1.png", "html");
});

casper.run();
```

And now we get a smaller image.

A typical usage of the capture methods is obviously **debugging**; when we do not know why our CasperJS is not working as expected, before spending time logging everything or inspecting all the elements, a simple screenshot might show us that we just forgot to perform a valid authentication due to which we are still blocked at the login page.

Another interesting usage is **documentation**. Writing a good user manual often involves inserting a lot of screenshots. Producing these screenshots can be quite long and painful, and it will be even more painful when we have to update them because the design may have changed since the last time we published the user manual.

So, how about using CasperJS to generate all the screenshots we need automatically from the current version of our web application? The principle is simple: we write a CasperJS script that reproduces the usage scenarios described in our documentation, we obtain a set of images, and we fuse them with our documentation text. Markdown, reStructuredText4, Textile, or similar formats are good candidates.

Resurrectio (see the *Getting started with CasperJS (Simple)* section) proposes to export any recorded sequence in two versions: a CasperJS version (which has our actual test scripts) and a reStructuredText version (which only contains comments and screenshots).

So we can run the test, obtain the screenshots, and compile our reStructuredText (with `rst2html`, `rst2doc`, `rst2pdf`, or so on) to get our document. Every time the design changes, we just re-run the test, recompile the text, and the document is updated automatically.

We can also use the capture methods from dynamically generated rendering to *produce static contents*.

For instance, if we use **d3.js** (`http://d3js.org/`) to draw gorgeous charts on our web page but would like to insert them in a newsletter or allow an old web browser to see them, we can turn them into images using CasperJS.

Let's take the following example from the `d3js.org` tutorial (`example15.html`):

```html
<html>
<head>
<style>
body {
  font: 10px sans-serif;
  color: white;
}
.arc path {
  stroke: #fff;
}
.arc text {
  fill: #fff;
}
</style>
</head>
<body>
<script src="http://d3js.org/d3.v3.min.js"></script>
<script>
var width = 400,
```

```javascript
    height = 200,
    radius = Math.min(width, height) / 2;

var color = d3.scale.ordinal()
    .range(["#98abc5", "#8a89a6", "#7b6888", "#6b486b", "#a05d56",
"#d0743c", "#ff8c00"]);

var arc = d3.svg.arc()
    .outerRadius(radius - 10)
    .innerRadius(radius - 70);

var pie = d3.layout.pie()
    .sort(null)
    .value(function(d) { return d.population; });

var svg = d3.select("body").append("svg")
    .attr("width", width)
    .attr("height", height)
  .append("g")
    .attr("transform", "translate(" + width / 2 + "," + height / 2 +
")");

d3.csv("data.csv", function(error, data) {

  data.forEach(function(d) {
    d.population = +d.population;
  });

  var g = svg.selectAll(".arc")
      .data(pie(data))
    .enter().append("g")
      .attr("class", "arc");

  g.append("path")
      .attr("d", arc)
      .style("fill", function(d) { return color(d.data.age); });

  g.append("text")
      .attr("transform", function(d) { return "translate(" + arc.
centroid(d) + ")"; })
      .attr("dy", ".35em")
      .style("text-anchor", "middle")
      .text(function(d) { return d.data.age; });
});
```

```
</script>
</body>
</html>
```

It reads a CSV file that contains population by age group and draws a donut chart using SVG.

Let's provide the needed data (`data.csv`):

```
age,population
<5,2704659
5-13,4499890
14-17,2159981
18-24,3853788
25-44,14106543
45-64,8819342
≥65,612463
```

Now we can launch our simple HTTP server and have a look. It will work well if we are using Chrome, for instance, but won't work with Internet Explorer 8.

CasperJS can be used to capture this chart so we can serve an equivalent image to the web browser that is not able to render SVG (`example15.js`):

```
var casper = require('casper').create();

casper.start('http://localhost:8000/example15.html');

casper.then(function() {
    this.captureSelector("chart.png", 'svg');
});

casper.run();
```

And the following is what we get:

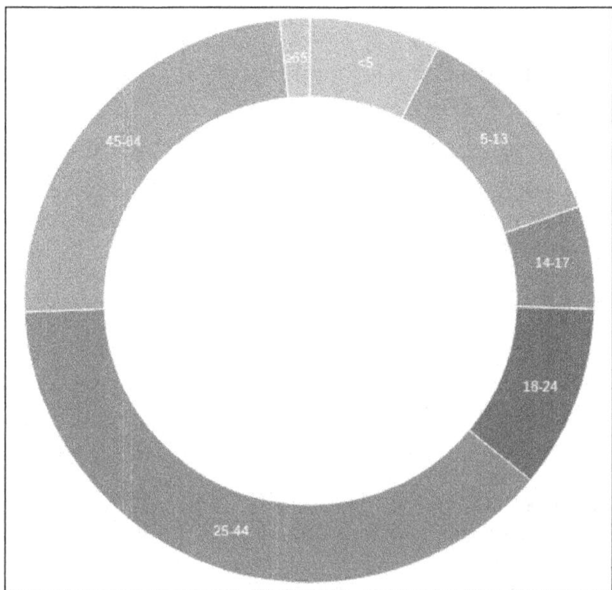

CasperJS can also be a smart way to provide a **server-side printing service**.

When we want our users to print our web pages, the most common and simple approach for them to use would be the web browser `print` feature. If we need to customize the rendering for printing (hide the navigation bar, change some colors or fonts, and so on), we can easily do so using a specific CSS for print (by mentioning `media="print"` inside the `link` tag). However, sometimes this is not enough.

Background images are a typical instance of where standard printing can be annoying; background images are hidden during printing, and it makes sense as we prefer to print text on a white background. But if we use them for a specific goal, such as filling the different bars of a bar chart, the printed result will be disappointing. (In our case, all the bars will be white, so we will not be able to distinguish between them.)

We will also have problems when we want to change the displayed information between screen and print. For instance, our page might contain a map with few markers. On the screen, we display a label when the mouse goes over a marker, but on print, we would prefer that all the labels are displayed.

In these problematic cases, a good solution is to use CasperJS as a **backend printing service**. The purpose is to highlight a service that takes as a parameter any URL, which returns an image capture of the corresponding page ready to be printed.

Our service will simply run a CasperJS script that will open the provided URL and then capture it:

```javascript
var casper = require('casper').create();
var url = casper.cli.options['targeturl'];
var output = casper.cli.options['outputfile'];

casper.start(url);

casper.then(function() {
    this.capture(output);
});

casper.run();
```

As we cannot use the `media="print"` attribute to apply some print-specific CSS (as CasperJS will open the page in the screen mode), we can dynamically add a specific class on the body element before capturing so we can easily style the rendering:

```javascript
casper.thenEvaluate(function () {
  var bodyclass = document.querySelector('body').
getAttribute('class');
  bodyclass = bodyclass + " print-mode";
  document.querySelector('body').setAttribute('class', bodyclass);
});
```

And if we want to allow a specific process to be performed before capturing (such as displaying all the marker labels on a map as discussed before), we might wait for a specific selector to be available. The list of selectors is as follows:

- In our target page, we add a JavaScript in charge of setting up the page for printing and adding a marker class on the `body` element as desired:

  ```javascript
  if (location.search.indexOf("print") > -1) {
    set_up_as_expected();
    document.querySelector('body').className += " ready-for-
  printing";
  }
  ```

- In CasperJS, we wait for this marker class to appear before capturing the output:

  ```javascript
  casper.waitForSelector(".ready-for-printing", function() {
      capture(this, selector, output);
  });
  ```

This service can be implemented with any web framework (we just need to be able to make a system call to run our CasperJS script).

Django Screamshot is a Django implementation and can be found at `https://github.com/makinacorpus/django-screamshot`.

About Packt Publishing

Packt, pronounced 'packed', published its first book "*Mastering phpMyAdmin for Effective MySQL Management*" in April 2004 and subsequently continued to specialize in publishing highly focused books on specific technologies and solutions.

Our books and publications share the experiences of your fellow IT professionals in adapting and customizing today's systems, applications, and frameworks. Our solution based books give you the knowledge and power to customize the software and technologies you're using to get the job done. Packt books are more specific and less general than the IT books you have seen in the past. Our unique business model allows us to bring you more focused information, giving you more of what you need to know, and less of what you don't.

Packt is a modern, yet unique publishing company, which focuses on producing quality, cutting-edge books for communities of developers, administrators, and newbies alike. For more information, please visit our website: `www.packtpub.com`.

Writing for Packt

We welcome all inquiries from people who are interested in authoring. Book proposals should be sent to `author@packtpub.com`. If your book idea is still at an early stage and you would like to discuss it first before writing a formal book proposal, contact us; one of our commissioning editors will get in touch with you.

We're not just looking for published authors; if you have strong technical skills but no writing experience, our experienced editors can help you develop a writing career, or simply get some additional reward for your expertise.

Instant Testing with QUnit

ISBN: 978-1-78328-217-3   Paperback: 64 pages

Employ QUnit to increase your efficiency when testing JavaScript code

1. Learn something new in an Instant! A short, fast, focused guide delivering immediate results

2. Learn about cross-browser testing with QUnit

3. Learn how to use popular QUnit plugins and develop your own plugins

4. Hands-on examples on all the essential QUnit methods

JavaScript Unit Testing

ISBN: 978-1-78216-062-5   Paperback: 190 pages

Your comprehensive and practical guide to efficiently performing and automating JavaScript unit testing

1. Learn and understand, using practical examples, synchronous and asynchronous JavaScript unit testing

2. Cover the most popular JavaScript Unit Testing Frameworks including Jasmine, YUITest, QUnit, and JsTestDriver

3. Automate and integrate your JavaScript Unit Testing for ease and efficiency

Please check **www.PacktPub.com** for information on our titles

9 781783 289431